Copyright © 2021 by Lola Muhammad

All rights reserved. No part of this book may be reproduced or used in any manner without written permission of the copyright owner except for the use of quotations in a book review. For more information, address: BOBAcademy@yahoo.com

FIRST EDITION
Print Hardback ISBN 978-1-7369629-0-9
Print Paperback ISBN 978-1-7369629-2-3
eBook ISBN 978-1-7369629-1-6

Instagram: B. O. B. Academy
Facebook: B O B Academy

Welcome to B.O.B. Academy where children of all ages can learn about the science of

BUSINESS.

What do you know about business?

First, we need to know and understand what a business is. You have probably seen many businesses but didn't know it. Any store, coffee shop, and even hospital you see, is a

BUSINESS.

WHAT IS A BUSINESS?

A business is any number of activities performed by people to either sell or produce services or products. This can be done from many places, including buildings and on the internet.

Have you or your parents made a purchase on the internet before?

What are products and services?

Products are physical items. Services are skills or time. For example, selling a piano is selling a product because the piano is a physical thing that can be touched. Selling piano lessons is selling a service because a skill is being taught and the seller is taking time to teach the skill.

Can you name a product you would like to sell? How about a service?

DID YOU KNOW THAT THERE ARE DIFFERENT TYPES OF BUSINESSES?

These are called business structures. Businesses are structured in a variety of ways. One is called a sole proprietorship (pruh-pry-i-ter-ship). That's a business that has only one owner. A fun way to remember that is in the word "sole", which means "the only one".

PARTNERSHIP

A partnership is when a business has two or more owners, who are called co-owners. The co-owners usually share in the profit and loss of the business.

What is a profit? A profit is the money a business gains which does not have to be spent on things the business needs.

15

EXAMPLE

An example is if you own a bakery and sell pie. You spend four dollars on the ingredients to bake the pie.

When you're finished baking, you sell it to a customer for ten dollars. Since you plan on baking more pie, you will take four dollars from what the customer gave you, to buy more ingredients. That leaves you with six dollars. The six dollars is your profit.

$10 - 4 = 6$

WHAT IS A LOSS?

What if nobody buys the pie from your store and the pie goes bad? Now you have to throw the pie away. Since you have spent four dollars on ingredients to bake the pie, but didn't make any money from the pie, it becomes a loss.

Do you think businesses prefer a profit or a loss?

CORPORATION

A corporation (kor-puh-ray-shun) is when a group of people are owners of a business but hire others to run and manage the
business. The owners share in the profit and loss, but the
responsibility of the company falls on the people who they have hired to manage it. Because of this, even the owners would be considered employees if they were to work for the corporation.

LLC

A Limited Liability (ly-uh-bil-i-tee) Company is called an LLC for short. An LLC is a mix between all of the
business stuctures mentioned earlier. There can be one or more owners and they can manage the business or choose to hire others to manage it. If the LLC ever owes someone money, the
owner does not have to use their own money to pay it back. Instead, the owner will use the money that the LLC has earned.

What similarities does an LLC have with the other business structures?

Now you know about the different types of businesses to choose from, but it's important to choose the one that is best for you.

Which type of business would you prefer? Why?

FUN FACT

Most Black-owned businesses sell a type of service instead of products.

ABOUT THE AUTHOR

Lola Muhammad is the author of the Black-owned Business (B.O.B.) Academy series. She has an MBA (Master of Business Administration degree) and completed her MBA Capstone Business Simulation, achieving a ranking in the top ten percentile in the country. She also has certificates in Project Management and Lean Six Sigma, while being a member of the National Black MBA Association (NBMBAA).

Lola has worked with children for over fifteen years and has three children of her own. She understands the importance of business and places value on learning the science of it at an early age.